Opposite Views

Some of these poems have appeared in the
New Statesman and *Best of SF*, Nos. 5 and 6

Opposite Views

Lawrence Sail

J. M. Dent & Sons Ltd · London

First published 1974
© Lawrence Sail 1971 ('Fisherman' and 'Expatriate teacher'),
1973 ('Cymbal player' and 'Report from planet Proteus'), 1974
All rights reserved. No part of this
publication may be reproduced, stored
in a retrieval system, or transmitted,
in any form or by any means, electronic,
mechanical, photocopying, recording or
otherwise, without the prior permission
of J.M. Dent & Sons Ltd.

Made in Great Britain
Printed by Lewis Reprints Ltd. Tonbridge
for
J.M. DENT & SONS LTD
Aldine House . Albemarle Street . London

If bound as a paperback, this book is subject to the condition
that it may not be issued on loan or otherwise except in its
original binding.

This book is set in 11/12 pt Press Roman

ISBN 0 460 02149 4

CONTENTS

For my mother

HOMECOMING

Grandparents, uncles, aunts — all gained in time
The same sad eyes, shrinking in hurt as I strayed
Beyond their comprehension: eyes cast down
Or painfully refocussed somewhere else,
Unable to outmanœuvre their lasting hope.

The statutory links alone survived
My growing up — an unconvincing perspective
Of greetings cards and automatic enquiries
Related to health or weather: and the rare meeting
Due to third parties, a marriage, birth or death.

Now, to my surprise, I am more and more
Composed of their gestures, an easy heir to habits
Long ago dismissed as the alien symbols
Of elderly minds. Too late I learn to trace
The common ground from which they tried to save me.

And perhaps this is the only natural way —
To find, long after, an uncle's forgotten gesture
Forming at one's own arm; an aunt's grimace
Masking the mirror; or my son's anxious eyes
Not understanding, watching as I look away.

SCHOOL DRIVER

After the last farewell, the last
Timely word of caution, they run
The few free yards from door to door —
A girl, three boys. Behind my shoulder
They settle with fuss, grouping themselves
At the edge of the mirror, as if for a picture:
Composed now, waiting to move forward.

All the way they chatter madly,
Comparing gifts — for they never travel
Empty-handed, but bear tribute
From one authority to another.
One day it was holly leaves
The school demanded: and once it was
A certain amount of raw wool.

Today they discussed in joyous detail
The sudden death of a budgerigar —
Not just finding it, though they made much
Of the oily feathers and upturned claws —
But what it could feel like, to fall and die
Behind bars, in a room not your own
Full of smoke and stale bird tunes.

I wanted then to turn and tell them
Of deaths slower than they could dream:
How they too had started that life-long
Glide to earth. But lacking status
Could only watch as they disappeared,
Feathers in hand, obediently passing
Into the silence of rooms not their own.

EXPATRIATE TEACHER

I bring you the symbols of alien gods
From Northern kingdoms weathered by the wind,
Where history lingers, though long ago destroyed
By word and war, by shapely post-war words.

I tell you of illuminated scripts,
The Roman Forum, the statues at Versailles:
Our tendency to build elaborate forms
Beyond our substance, outliving time and pain.

You walk to school barefoot, on stony paths;
By wind-sharp thorn you see the jackal move,
Biding its time. At night the cattle shift
Uneasily beneath the sullen moon.

What use are books and marble, when the senses
Go numb and fail to warn of coming danger?
At home you shed your blazer, casting off
The Latin motto they stitched across your heart.

WATER GARDEN MIRAGE
(for W.G. Moore)

Safely from the terrace I admire
The clever obstacles, the swift disguises —
Water, polished hard by sunlight, which flowers
In liquid fleurs-de-lys, or flames in candles;
Which leaves damp grottos thick with confidences;
Which gushes out from gaping lips of stone.
Words of water used and used again.

Drawn forward, I follow the falling stairs
Escorted by rails which twist by at my elbow,
Down to islands of laurel and towering cypress,
Narrow causeways of gravel. Allowing myself
The indulgent smile of hindsight, I consider
The garden's maker — a childish delight, after all,
Such tampering with water. Or was it the climate?

Reaching the central lake, I stand alone
Half hypnotized by its sleek surface, half seeing
Water-lilies slowly revolve, revolve.
Receding voices merge with the thickness of water —
Not threatening, I tell myself, just softer,
Like voices which dissolve across a darkness.
There is, I tell myself, no need to panic.

Or is it the climate? I feel the heat in my throat,
Acid sweat stars my eyes. Groping for water
I find only candles, flowers, the same old words
Spewed onto green rock: and now, remember
The cool basin with its bright button of brass
At the top of the stairs, at the top of the waterfall,
Up on the terrace of blank, cascading water.

PERSPECTIVE

The milkman knocked last week to say
No more bottles would be delivered,
For he had seen how nothing mattered
When set beside the Milky Way.

The newspaperman apologized
But said his service had to end:
Through rolled-up tubes of print he'd spied
The helplessness of human lives.

The meter ticked on, remained unread,
Until the board sent up their man —
Only to tell us that in all the stars
He could find no spark to light the dead.

While we sat on the empty terrace
The baker arrived with a loaf so crisp
That it cracked at a touch. As we broke and ate,
The galaxies fell quietly into place.

ENTERING THE CITY

Last free field of sprawling thistle,
Last shop crammed with dusty sweet-jars,
Soap, paper, milk and carrots,
Last house standing alone, filed down
By sky on either side.

Last hedge with nothing to hide
But corn and a random number of nests
Unapproved by prim committees,
Last woodland fermenting wild flowers,
Last country living.

Last touch of hand and water,
Last glimpse of earth meeting sky,
Railway siding landscaped with coal,
Hoardings high over bombsite brambles,
Name and coat of arms.

First playground beyond black railings,
First long terrace trudging downhill,
Sodium flaring from concrete stems,
Municipal lorries loaded with plants:
The first hollow pavement begins.

MIGRANTS

Midnight. Wheels still squeal in the lane.
Further up the coast, the lay-bys
Will be blockaded with caravans, cars,
Dinghies, dormobiles, trucks and trailers:
Estates of nomads improvising sleep,
Their minds awash in tides of passing lights.

For others keep on, unwilling to lose
Except for petrol, tea, a smoke,
A pee, a gulp of fatty air,
A moment. They postpone their dreams
Till, parked in rows along the front, they let
The dimly shifting ocean lull them loose.

Behind them dust resettles, calm
Laps through their curtained houses, clearing
A year's flotsam. Journeying on
They head for home: new letters dealt
Untidily across the hall, and beyond,
The kindly futures of those sea-swept rooms.

POEM FOR A BLIND MAN

Written words are not much use
Unless above the normal level:
Even when spoken, many must pass
Flatly into your mind and die.
Mostly these are warnings, mid-
Course corrections, kindly meant
But curt, not wanting to condescend —
Kerb, one step to go, watch out
For the backswing of branch or sprung door.

So often I have wished for you words
Succulent, dribbling juice like steak,
Syllables lasting like spring bells
In an empty valley: words of velvet,
Leather, silk, tree-bark, crystal
For you to feel, taste, possess.
Each morning to your fine fingertips
I would guide vowels comose as peaches,
Consonants craggy as chipped rock.

It needs your gentle smile to remind me
How many worlds of sound and surface
Daily surround you: changes of gear,
High voices, low voices, clocks and knives,
Birdsong, grass unbending, the wind
Describing what it passes through:
The softness of hands and the shock of steel.
All these reshape your mind's old words,
Focussing them in acute dimensions.

FIRST LESSON

I am holding it up like this
so that you all can see it:
you've seen it often, I'm sure
in the meadows where you play
or by the road.

And now, watch, as I strip
one by one, the petals:
I'm doing this to show
how even a flower has secrets
and complex workings.

Note the stamen, comprising
filament and anther. Inside
we find the pistil, consisting
of ovaries, stigma and style.
Remember these words.

What is your question? Ah, those
are ovules, fertilized
by pollen — a brief affair
of bees and falling powder
which does not concern us.

So next time you see a flower,
children, don't simply think
how pretty it looks, but try
applying these grown-up words.
And watch it die.

REPORT FROM THE PLANET PROTEUS

They have arrived — at last! and, as we feared,
In nothing better than a brittle box of metal
Crammed with outmoded data. I could hardly believe
The shock transmitted by my regolith,
The rigid impact of their primitive craft
Thudding, juddering down.

I haven't the heart or, come to that, the language
To tell them that their cargo of rattling digits
And slick equations will serve no purpose here.
In the end, of course, they're bound to notice
  something —
The way their footprints fade, horizons shift,
All measurements misfit.

I've done my best for them, supplied a ledge
Of solid rock, a layer of purple dust —
Even a hillock flared with astroblemes.
I only hope it lasts, because I sense
A growing impulse in that very region
Towards a methane sea.

There is, for once, no choice: we must allow
Their stunted minds to glean at least a semblance
Of so-called 'facts'. They are not ready yet
To do without the security of selection.
Here's hoping that gamma nine can stabilize
Enough to suggest a moon.

Let them return to earth, report their findings:
Distortion protects us, they will not find us again,
Or know us even if they did. One distant day
They too may learn to live as multiforms —
Till then our possible orbits, fellow planets
Laughingly ring their science.

INDECISION

I keep on half-wanting to go outside, where snowdrops
Come bursting through winter; to escape
The unformed whiteness of paper
And the no-nonsense angles of walls,
To sit by a gesturing tree with just the right book —
Posing, as memory sketches the tranquil moment.

But once outside, I would keep on half-wanting to creep
Upstairs to the well-drilled books,
The calm shadows of this room
Overlooking the garden:
Up the stairs where the mark of my turning heel
Has scored the wood with circles, circles, circles.

DEATH OF A CHILD

It lay beyond the tidy garden ways —
An endless world where wicked berries gleamed
Precisely in the seasonless disorder;
With leaves like flags hoisted to dizzy treetops,
Cables of creeper a foot thick. A place
Where nothing was settled, nothing tamely focussed
To prim gravel, a few labelled roses.
He noticed that this area shared with others
The name of 'no', selected by his parents.

The parents, who often later blamed themselves,
Smiled as he tested boundaries through four summers.
The potting shed was good while it lasted, the trees
Easily bore his weight — and, when those palled,
It was time to help him make his own small garden:
A replica of father's, ten feet square,
With regular rows and room to walk between.
He liked it when they knelt to dig his garden,
Seeing behind their heads the great space no.

In the fifth year, beneath the splaying orchids,
The opposite view had equal fascination —
Looking back, he could barely define the zone
Of barren ground in which his parents stooped,
Peering, calling, anxious to know where he was.
But he was no, all made of shiny tubers,
With berry eyes and skin smooth as leaves,
Twigs for fingers and a dark mind. In delight
He shouted his name, fled down the unfenced ways.

And when, breathless, he paused, it seemed to him
He stood at his own true threshold — a cool clearing
Of grass and lily flowers, at whose still centre
Bamboo had formed a graceful canopy.
The light still held, he had only to cross.
From the first step forward, he felt the ground give way
In recognition: boldly, with joy, he trod
Into the reed-covered lake. They found him there,
His eyes still bright, staring beyond their world.

And here they are again, collecting shells.
They often do things like that. Look at their heads:
Good heads, I think. They are bending over the pool.
They love their father. In winter he also goes with them,
Makes animals by packing the frozen snow.

Here, in fact, is a rabbit. Isn't it good?
And now, a bear — the polar kind, of course —
It really looks as if it will fall and smother
All the family. He's clever with his hands
My son. I think he's doing very well.

Each year he sends me pictures such as these:
I keep them for the longer winter evenings.
Sometimes, at night, I see my grandchildren's faces
Right above me — their pale blue eyes which peer
Calmly into the stillness where I live.

CHALLENGE

Who demanded order? demand the trees
Beyond the window, shaking fistfuls of leaves,
Damp, green fingers clamped to the glass.

Who cleared the garden? brag the fertile weeds,
Chipping in between flaking stone to extend
Succulent shoots to the garden's end.

Who hoped for harvest? enquires the rubbery slug,
Smugly mouthing his words through a smother of green
Which might have become lettuce, or beans.

Some impulse which I do not understand
Provokes me to search the house from cellar to roof
For powders, saw and spade — a token proof.

ANNIVERSARY

'Not these ones: those.' The flowers he will not see
Must be long-lasting. Solemnly you select
Unripe tulips weatherboarded in green,
Daffodils which bow their fisted buds.

Declining a cellophane shroud, we trudge along
The ritual paths, where just a year ago
Aunts and uncles paraded, their faces wired
In stiff arrangements of official grief.

Now you have some trouble finding the spot,
Forgetting he is no more at the end of a row.
But nothing can deter you: with missionary zeal
You track down death, armed with your paltry spring.

You stoop, fan out the stalks along his chest:
The leaves squeak as you handle them, then lie
Prone, rootless, ears to the hollow ground.
Rain begins. The scattered buds creak open.

As we drive home, the wipers fail to staunch
Your spikenard tears. Hunched at the wheel, I hear
Angry bells blockading my brain, as if
You had left an alarm clock, set for judgement day.

ADJUSTMENT

Another one dying, not five yards away —
A wrinkled suit, slowly deflating
As blood disperses through level streets;
Shoes vertical, massive as skis,
Stubbing their toes against cut stone.

Each focussed detail should scream in the mind,
Hairs which the razor missed that morning,
Breast-pocket biro, ring on stiff finger:
Perhaps there are letters in one of the pockets,
A picture even? Relax, it's a body.

Besides, the experts will soon arrive
To comfort the broken-hearted, explain
The basic trends and historical reasons —
Wise and gentle men, intoning
The litany of the accepted fact.

Helpless we watch, bewitched by the constant
Seepage of life — so numb with sensation
That it's only our dad who leaps up in alarm
To adjust the sensitive tuner, growling:
'That's never the colour of real blood.'

SLOW REWIND

The door which was closed flies open as you leave,
Magic triggers the gate behind your back:
And she reappears, sleepwalking into your arms.

Now in the lanes
You reverse at speed uphill
The fields beyond your screen
Grow wider, smaller,
Multiplying to a landscape.
Triumphant you ride the horizon
Together heading home
Over the sunlit ridge
Towards what might have been.

A leap from the car
And your magnetized feet
One two one two
Jerk you away
To the waiting door.
Over the threshold
Into the warm
You hop in turn,
The door slams shut.

You sit, staring at the blank square of wall,
Trying to readjust to the world going on,
Fooled for a time by your anti-clockwise spell.

CYMBAL PLAYER

after all that time
a lifetime perhaps
of watching the others
their brute bulged cheeks
swift spiky fingers
oceans of slow arms

at last he holds
gingerly these
brackets of gold
to trap the earth in
stealthily now he
raises them high and

light lashes the seas
flashing the world blind
he   god   lasts a whole
second   now awaits
the long lurch homewards
across the splintered planet

AT THE CINEMA

After that opening scene in the cobwebbed wood
Where Death, tophatted, steers his curtained carriage,
We guess the rest: the desecrated grave,
Suspicious servants, doors with un-oiled hinges.
On later reels the long-toothed count himself,
Exposed by lightning against a mullioned window,
Crouches, his connoisseur's eye intent on breasts
Bulbous as beachballs. Blood on stone. Effects.
The final chase — one pair of breasts too many
Transfixes the villain, just in the nipple of time.

The lights go up. Reluctantly we leave
Horror so safely screened by old conventions —
Outside, the empty city waits in ambush,
Each blackened angle honed to razor sharpness.

AFTER INDEPENDENCE

Testily you lurch forward from day to day,
Cursing governments long since superseded,
Enraged by your wife's long-suffering calm, who knows
Your need for scapegoats and still has plans for
  a future.

No good explaining now, in black and white,
The unpolitical hopes with which you came —
To contract teachers, diplomats, engineers,
Or self-important envoys out from London.

Nobody left has time or inclination
To hear of oxcarts bouncing inland, despite
Rivers, boulders, lack of food and drugs,
The trial and error of each slogging footstep;

Or of the ground cleared, the hard bargains
Struck with recalcitrant chiefs, the first failed
  crops,
Pigs and sheep nursed through the alien weather —
Everything improvised out of very little.

The water has been bridged, disease overcome,
Level tarmac marches far upcountry;
Well-drilled villas wheel across the valleys,
Housing the families of ambitious clerks.

For you there's nothing left but baffled anger
Urging you on to mine the city, dismantle
Supermarkets and tower blocks, restore
The hills to wildness, pepper the lakes with birds.

It's never occurred to you that one house built
Might cause, in time, a city; each acre fenced
Create indignant neighbours; or a bargain struck
Easily lead to demands for equal terms.

So you live on, besieged by forms, conditions,
The threat of unpaid eavesdroppers: knowing your
  presence
Tolerated at best, your past condoned
Though textbooks have already turned against you.

The old simplicity's gone. Your sons attend
Multiracial schools — will emigrate
To Europe once again, as aliens, or
After their father's death, even as settlers.

TIGHTROPE WALKER

On either side below, blank mouths
Form 'fall'. Glittering dots of eyes
Mirror his body, derailed and splayed.
In each provincial town he finds —
After the tumblers and baggy clowns,
After the false alarm of drums —
This same sad sea of upturned faces
Inviting disaster.

Ahead, the twisting strand of silver
Tingles, a live nerve. One step
Forward shocks the next foot forward:
Acutely he feels each muscle contract,
Each fingertip minutely measure
His thin balance. Foot by foot
He tests his stance.Inch by inch
His heart quickens.

Halfway over. He wobbles, jerks at the
Waist as if winded. His sequined tights
Shiver with lights. Circling arms
Beat air, knees buckle. Children hide
Their faces, adults gasp — then smile
Sheepishly, as he straightens up.
Of course, how silly, it's all a part
Of old routines.

Behind him the line loops slack, he has
Six feet to go — and after that?
Applause, the slow climb earthwards, then
Through mud, on duckboards, back to bed,
Back to tomorrow. Three feet more.
He reaches out to grasp safe rails,
Lands on solid wood and feels
The world go dead.

FISHERMAN

Out past the twinkling land there rides a craft,
Hove to and steeply rocking in the sea.
One barely glimpsed, at paying out the nets
Which all his life have been his life, reflects
How many nights like this one have washed aft
As silently as tides flood in and flee.

But as he reaches to clear the tarry strands
He sees the water, black beyond his hands
And pauses. Rough hands grasping at his own
Pull steadily, not inwards now but down.

MORE GOOD NEWS

The age of terror is past! Instead
We offer, my lords and ladies, this —
The well-lit era of information
Exploding the maze from A to Z.

Let me explain, in confidence,
The findings of our great committee
In which, I hasten to add, you'll find
No single point of dissidence.

Fear, and the experts all agree,
Is a windy night, a darkened room,
The gunbolt bedded into the breech,
Slow footsteps on gravel or scree:

Fear is the time before knowledge comes
And the moment at which it dissolves to nothing;
Fear is the enemy closing in
When spittle dries against the gums.

But today all that is over! We know,
Each one of us, what a bullet-hole looks like,
How people run, the way a mother
Shields her child from the rifle-butt blow.

Bombs serenely gliding through air,
Tanks, machine-guns: these are nothing
More than familiar sights, brought home
Faithfully by the camera's stare.

Nothing need happen by fate or chance.
Now that the future has also been planned.
Your every move between here and death
Is public knowledge decades in advance.

So you see there's no need for horoscopes,
Or sudden alarm. No mystery
Can tug at your heart, no unreal dream
Bring you back to the terror of hope.

ONE OF THE UNFIT

You lie lassoed, within the mountain's shadow,
By the grey tide which smothered you, from behind —
And you didn't even run.

Nothing but a periscope horn, driving forward
To plough the sulphur and siphon down old codes
For your silted brain — the tang of the desert rose,
The long dust of the herd heading for water,
Suns and moons breaking above your head.
This and a ripple of ribs just breaking surface
Deft scavengers have polished, ashes preserved.

The brain was always limited, confined
Short of the plain's horizon, warped by heat —
Even immediate vision blurred with flies.
Danger could only assume a known form,
Low as a lion, or between the hyena's sprung jaws.
But this? The earth gave food, it was nothing more
Than sweet, white grass, memento and promise of rain.

I see you fatally lamed by disbelief,
Scarcely feeling the scalding flow round your ankles
As the grey tide overtook you.

AT SIX MONTHS

Six months — already a legend made of one
Journey through night and rain,
Portents of pain and the miracle seizure which brought
The blood-caked head to surface in white walls:
For this was your first, your lasting definition.

Too quickly others followed: names, comparisons
With aunts and uncles, cousins.
Your every move is noted, each new habit
Attributed to throw-back or the dead:
Whole dynasties of pride explain you away.

Already your slow revenge has started — the first
Tooth breaking the gum.
And this is only a start, the innocent prelude
To independence: the power to choose your words
Cunningly, so that every syllable stings.

You will not then forgive the stories told
By sentimental warders
Recalling the night they built a family round you:
Nor understand your mother's haggard face
Until once more you stand on the threshold of silence.

LEGACY

The pictures are left and most of all that subject
You painted so often, of broad-ribbed boats on a shore.
No pleasure-boats, these, to bob by planks on wheels,
But massive, made from the memories of storms,
Deeply rooted far in the sand's dry depths.

Not once did you face them seaward, paint in canvas,
Or bring the flickering foam to lift their bows.

And then that island — in early versions it lay
Like a misplaced cloud across the even water;
So light it would surely lift and drift with the first
Fine wind. Later it swelled to a chalky scarp
Became treacherous, acquired a hostile summit.

There were never people or houses on your island:
Blank as an iceberg, it cut clean through horizons.

In time, the boats climbed higher up the beach;
No tide could touch them, not even one freak breaker
Reclaim their hulking walls. And all this while
The island grew, diminishing sea and sky,
Yet always drifting further out of reach.

I often think how through thirty years of marriage,
War and remarriage, you illustrated defeat.

WIDOW'S ROUTINE

It took not quite a year
To gauge the length of a day, prevent surprise
Attacks by shadows and learn to crack an egg
Without minding the echo returned by the house.
Getting up late was quite a help, she maintained,
Sadly smiling.

Breakfast at noon implied
Lunch at three, a little something at seven;
And dinner, what with cooking and preparing,
Could hardly be ready for some time after that.
This, she explained, was no idle affectation,
Just preference.

Then there was the garden —
Flowers to be tended, weeds to disengage,
Not to mention a cat to be fed and talked to,
Letters to write, the occasional game of cards.
Never, she said, had she been so completely busy,
Brightly smiling.

And if, after all, there remained
Some time still unaccounted for, she could
Always slip upstairs and, by the mirror,
Retrace the contours of her smiling lips.
Not, as she told herself, for reassurance,
Just vanity.

APART

'I have made the chicken last through a fourth day.
There is no panic. The washing will soon get done
The draining-board is clear. Nothing has happened.'
Each evening when you ring, I make the effort
To sound unruffled — just as you also sound
From a hundred miles away; your voice so gentle
It seems you are afraid to bruise my eardrum.

When our words drift over counties, nothing is hard —
Affections jam the exchange, extravagant silence
Becomes a gift to distribute in between words.
We span the dangerous distance with tokens of love:
In case the car should crash, the aeroplane fly
Too near the sun, the survivor have to face
The end of pride, beginnings of a conscience.

With mouth and ear alone we bring about
A miracle of intimate relations.
Invisibly we blossom, you becoming
The perfect wife I always knew you were,
While I send forests of flowers to where you're staying
And think how lucky I am, recalling my mother
Boiling an egg for her supper, again and again.

The day we do not speak, the house will look
Suddenly grubby, everything out of place,
Chicken-bones everywhere. Oversleeping, I'll wake
To hear the doorbell wrenched from its socket and just
Have time to dash downstairs, fumble the lock.
After that, the disappointment lasts
Only till both have forgotten and then remembered.

GUIDELINES

good afternoon and welcome come this way
here on the ground floor im sorry no dogs or prams
to your left the two imposing busts portray
the marquis and his wife they were executed
by bartolini yes they look content maam
as well they might do having instituted
eleven sons each with his monogram

the library contains twelve thousand tomes
mostly unread and thus in fine condition
while the famous tapestry hanging opposite comes
from bruges and shows us cupid as he cheers
two noble lovers on to coy coition
the fireplace of course is adam the chandelier
french one of the ninth earls acquisitions

the sofa here in the drawingroom was a gift
from catherine the great to the fourteenth count
dont miss the stuccoed ceiling here is the lift
installed by the national trust and made in preston
in nineteen thirty five here we dismount
to view the bedrooms continue our ingestion
of useless facts in staggering amounts

this fine fourposter the last heir occupied
a bishop who had it carved with every spire
within the diocese and later died
in italy from a painful stomach gout
to be precise in some poor peasants byre
who wouldnt house a heretic being devout
a turn of the wheel one cannot but admire

the rest you can see for yourselves the original lock
on the sixteenth century chest the silverware
sevres vases mirrors screens and clocks
untouched by hand roped off in holy precincts
dynastic gods preserved in musty air
note the virginal with its quite distinct
keyboard of nails and strings of human hair

our tour ends here for those of you who plan
a second visit dont forget a supply
of matches petrol even grenades if you can
youll find me waiting away from the house and drive
behind damp walls where my family serves and dies
after two hundred years still stubborn enough to survive
kept warm by a dream of flames climbing roofhigh

LANDFALL

No course of ours had steered to that inland state,
No special grace, or confluence of currents
Engineering new levels. Yet both of us —
You, with hair unwound on the moonwhite pillow,
Calmly taking my gaze; and I at last
Free of questions — knew we had never before,
Being seafarers, journeyed so far from water.

Later, I tried to piece the route together,
Searching in vain for clues — the day had passed
Much as another. Minor panics, doorbells,
A baby cutting teeth, a finger cut
And bandaged, nothing more. The usual rise
And usual fall of circumstance, which leave
Slowly evolving ruins along the shore.

It still disturbs me, that there should be no chart
Or tidy compass bearing, by which to locate
That island of ourselves above the litter
Marooned by daily tides. But slowly I'm learning
How love, like moonlight, may not be achieved —
Only, as in the ocean's timeless turning,
Be followed through its own slow rhythms and received.

PEBBLE STORY

It caught my eye — the brindled fruit
Of cold passages, firmly niched
In the stream's paved floor. A fossil of sunlight
Fallen from leaves, fish-still, fish-bright:
Far too tempting not to loot.

Out of the water, it gleamed in my palm,
Smaller than I had expected, but still
Well worth saving for its smooth skin,
And the feel it had of harbouring
A core of history, tightly embalmed.

Now, dull, collecting dust,
It lies cast up along my shelf —
Just a pebble I happened to meet,
The sort a dog might drop at your feet:
Meaningless. The colour of rust.

VINCENT AT AUVERS

Nothing needs to be done. I watch
pipesmoke flatten against the ceiling.
From time to time, footsteps approach
or voices consult, then fade away.

Lying here, it's strange to feel
the Doctor's borrowed cure at work —
relief from pain at last achieved
with a single anaesthetic shot.

Better this than the oncoming birds
bracketing under their black wings
the cornfields of my wild sea-province:
better this than the madness of hoping.

Outside, I know, the world is cooling,
taking on its old Dutch sense
of level fields ruled off by water,
windmills slicing the grey air.

I can hear the footsteps of miners, women
and well-meaning doctors, as they recede
down misty canals; endless echoes
drifting back through the endless distance.

Theo, you will understand
my lying here. And when you come,
nothing more will need to be done:
outside, the last sunflowers are fraying.

CURRICULUM VITAE

The evidence covers, if I am clever,
A page and a half: all that remains
Of thirty years, for official reading.
So few places, it seems, were ever
More than nodded past, receding
In damp and level acres from the passing train.

But even such tidy exhumations
Release, like madeleines dunked in tea,
Too many ghosts for this thin text —
Footnotes, errata, interpretations
Rioting under the palimpsest,
Each demanding the status of referee.

Schools with their coughing cisterns and clocks,
Parks at dusklight, toys and tears:
The corpse of childhood, disinterred,
Grows flesh again and runs amok,
Exploding the tidy work of words
With which I try to edit the heart's careers.

To which firm dates shall I commit
Friendship, music, the fine traps laid
By more than friendship? How explain
The power of sunsets? How omit
Landscapes locked inside the brain,
The seconds which make up each long decade?

Names and dates, a word or two —
All you require is the bare-boned proof
Of years outlived; a life confined
To the churchyard index of who was who.
So I'll keep the ghosts. At least they define
Survival into old age — or a lasting youth.

THE RETURN

This is the house to which you came back
After your mother died:
These the roseheads pitted with black,
Once her pride.

Here is the door through which you passed
Into the echoing hall
Where gleaming mercury trapped in glass
Predicted rainfall.

Up these stairs which she dusted and swept
Daily, you climbed to bed:
Beside your unwashed pillow, you kept
The book she read.

And this cracked mirror is one in which
Her image beckoned to you
The night they found you drowned in a ditch
Gazing through.

CONSUMER POEMS

conform to safety standards, have been rigorously
  checked,
are guaranteed free from deleterious side-effects,
will not harm pregnant women or play havoc with
  your purse,
leave children of all ages and both sexes none the
  worse,
won't remove your eyebrows, spoil your nails or
  aggravate
skin complaints and dandruff; are no danger to the
  State.
They're washable, unbreakable, hygienic, well
  designed,
non-iron, non-crease, non-toxic, non-inflammable,
  non-aligned.

But beware of imitations which have recently come to
  light,
inferior products marketed subversively at night.
Innocuous though they may at first appear, don't
  be deceived —
they are the work of undesirable elements, aggrieved
by lack of status or comfort: men who listen to the
  tides,
memorize the workings of flowers and loiter at the
  roadside.
Leave dangerous poems such as these unread — or
  else, by stealth,
a sense of hope could once again damage the
  national health.

TRANSLATION

From the rounded lump of clay
Weighting his arm, the potter dreams
Showcases ranged with neat displays
Of every shape he might ever mean
To make: can sense, in his spread hand,
Historic futures calmly spanned.

But clockwise, clockwise, turns the wheel,
Unwinding dreams. With sinking heart
He watches the cone rising, can feel
The pressure force his hands apart —
Another object, to be consigned
To dusty shelves at the back of his mind.

BETWEEN US

The words go to and fro between us,
Words we have used before:
Therefore, like any message re-read,
They are less than words and more.

Their etymology is simple,
Upshot of eight years of marriage —
Shared lives, divided meanings,
They bear our mirror image.

Now it is anger, danger, fear
Which best provoke our care:
Harder now for both to discover
The words which lay love bare.

Sometimes now you would rather stop
Short of difficult speech,
Opting instead for neutral silence
Out of history's reach.

But silence needs to be surrounded
Like a whole bar's rest,
Whose value only drums and trumpets
Know how to bring out best.

Only with words, my love, may we
Make silence precious, or enclose
Within the difference of our meanings
Love to living juxtaposed.

REVISED VERSION

A thundering expatriate prayer
Disperses through the morning air
Its well adjusted liturgies
Designed for new authorities:
For 'queen' we now read 'president',
'Commissioner' for 'resident' —
But prayer of sound and prayer of soul
Address themselves to different goals.

'God bless our chiefs and sub-locations'
(Our healthy and unhealthy stations)
'God bless our Church, which still serves on'
(Although the imperial troops have gone)
'And if it be Thy will, O Lord.
Protect Thy priests from fire and sword:
Lord, feed Thy sheep' (though black they be,
Enlighten them, of Thy charity).

'We thank Thee for Thy gifts of love'
(A golf course still, thank God above)
'We thank Thee for the world around'
(And more especially, for the cricket ground)
'Keep us this day all free from sin'
(And, Lord, let no Revolution begin)
'Amen, Amen again I say'
(Ah, white men, it's for you I pray).

AFTER WEIGHTLESSNESS

Once, the random sweep of an arm sufficed
To disperse planets like seedballs, rearrange
A galaxy. There were whole systems, then,
Bent round my clever thumb: and I could utter
Stars by the thousand, or laughingly banish light-
  years
Within the compass of my own spread fingers.

Since then, how many vengeful atmospheres
Have crushed my joints! Each pebble that I lift
Here on Earth, bruises the skin with blood,
Leaving its dark ring. Wherever I look,
Rivers hurtle seawards, unbalanced trees
Topple, helpless, towards the hidden centre.

Within me, now, I feel the fatal mass
Of dreams grown heavy, each imagined order
Compacted, bearing me down through clay and water:
And when, with effort, I raise my face to the mirror,
Each day, with growing terror I confront
Some-one else's definition of power.

SEQUEL

your eyes scan left to right between
the margins' limits, then back and one
notch down: as regular as a typewriter,
steady as breathing.

to bring you out of this lengthening spell
is almost impossible. farther and deeper
your obedient eyes conduct your mind
through walls of words.

deaf to conversation, immune
to fading light, you redefine
reality as the growing weight
of left-hand pages.

later, you'll peer to where i sit
across the darkened room, and wonder
to what shapeless story suddenly
you've been transferred:

and vaguely greet me, recognizing
some minor character, encountered
several chapters back, before
you lost your place.

A RUINED HOUSE

As you reached the turn of the path, it brought you up
Short, with a child's frown. You did not notice,
Perhaps, the undarned roof, the final Z
Nailed to the empty doorframe. Or perhaps you noticed
Other things — sunlight sharp on spikes of glass,
One last windlifted curtain: enough of privacy
To make you pause, look back. Or else you saw
All of this, and could not puzzle out
The sense locked up in one look's contradictions.

Inside, we found the instruments of surrender
Common to all defeated houses — a bottle,
Rags and rubble, the tramp's black square of floor.
Upstairs was a bed too broken to be removed,
Its mattress sagged like a corpse; and, along one wall,
A scroll of floral paper curling down
And inwards, inch by inch. As we emerged,
'Why?' you demanded. I heard your voice rebound
From room to room, disturbing the musty air.

I took you round to see the cowstalls sprung
With four-foot nettles; told you the yellow flower
Was stonecrop; lifted you up to let you tug
At ringbolts tethered along a crumbling wall.
But you persisted — 'What did they really do wrong?' —
As if it needed some evident misconduct
Or Greek miscalculation to explain
Such wrecking: instead of simply life on life,
Time's lasting inattention, lengthening odds.

Later, arriving home, you paused again
Beside the well-oiled gate, to peer at the house
Facing you at the end of the level garden:
Trim white paintwork, curtains at every window.

In future you would go more warily, knowing
That houses had rules of their own, were not to be
  trusted:
Any more than fathers who failed to answer
A simple question. Gently you slipped the catch
And went on ahead: this time, no backward look.

A PICTURE BY KLEE

X-rayed against the double night
Of the cut moon and the dwarf sun,
The wire frames of your skeleton town
Might have been gutted by fire, or nudged
Askew by earthquake.

But over the leaning towers, bright flags
Semaphore their messages
Of occupation, refuse to submit
To natural disaster, or
Random history.

No town was ever so ruined, or sited
So far beyond the reach of weather,
The limits of naming: yet each step taken
Along its deserted streets, provokes
Familiar echoes.

For this is the fossil Troy, embedded
In all our minds: the child's first sketch
Of heaven, the old man's Holy City,
Clear as glass. The first and last
Possible settlement.

ALTERNATIVES

In this house, today, I must face again
The consequences of that first betrayal:
The quick division of cells,
The envious opposite numbers
Which, since our birth, have counted out whole deserts
Between the brief oases of satisfaction.

Either, to stay behind these familiar doors,
Gathering data, wreaking no futher damage,
And teach myself in time
How to grow into the walls:
One day then, calmly to be absorbed
Into the fabric of my well-stocked tomb.

Or, bravely imperfect, to disperse along
This way or that, carpet-bag stuffed with patents,
In search of anonymous lakes,
Peaks undivided by names:
To become a mapper of mirages, an intimate
Of roadside verges, expert at meeting strangers.

Either, my heirs at last allowed to cross
Into the stuffy room where they lost a father:
Or further expeditions,
Pursued through generations,
Pushing a few yards on from that last failure
Of dilettante parents crazed by sun.

Either, or — in my father's house, I weigh
The mutually balanced forces of deduction.
And this is the worst fear:
To think how sons and fathers
Might cancel each other out, their warring minds
Fall to zero, for want of either madness.

A REPLY TO RECALCITRANT CITIZENS

With reference to your plea, the full Committee
Has carefully considered every clause
And, without prejudice to future laws,
Acknowledges the charm of your one, last city —
A quaint survival, exuding the musty air
Of churches and bookrooms through its archaic squares.

Further, it is agreed, from fellow-feeling,
That government shall make some small provision
For those too old or slow to face decisions
Required to stop our systems from congealing:
The state, as you must know, can always find
An embrocation for the unquiet mind.

Notwithstanding, however, such give and take,
Our central thesis, it seems to us, remains
Unchallenged (and rightly so, in view of the pains
We took to be elected, for your sakes):
Nor can we shirk our duty, to ensure
That men keep pace with progress more and more.

Besides, the evidence is clear — to wit,
Your suburbs hold up traffic, while at your centre
Cars lie rotting, unable to leave or enter,
Shoppers step off pavements, pedestrians flit
Everywhere. In short, your city poses
A threat to tidal flow as great as Moses.

Therefore, citizens, I must repeat
Committee's firm intention, namely, to approve
The motorway in full, and thus remove
A unit of living by now quite obsolete.
And remember, it is only destinations
Which stand in the way of improved communications.

AFTER THE REUNION

The following day, I saw you once more —
Making your way through thin rain
Past grey college walls, back to the train;
Suitcase in hand, your face gripped
By worry, as if something had slipped
Your mind, which memory could not restore.

Stopped by the lights, I watched you cross
A few feet ahead — forgetting that,
Even through glass, a stare attracts
Attention. You looked up, surprised,
And quickly down again, your eyes
Unwilling to focus nine years' loss.

'Christ! you had said at the dinner, 'It's great
To meet again!' — and out they came,
The stale old jokes, forgotten names,
River parties, escapades:
Your past, like college silver, displayed
Intact inside its walled estate.

You really did expect to trace
Those common threads, across the maze
Of marriage, children, jobs, decay —
And vainly I tried, as others did,
To fool you, nodded agreement and hid
Embarrassment under a smiling face.

Now, disappointed, you gave me this last
Reproving look. Then amber, green:
Tyremarks where your tracks had been.
Driving on, I wondered who
Had best played Judas, me or you:
You to the present, or I to the past.

APPROACHES TO THE SEA

The clifftop walker, taking the air,
Admires the sea: a distant view
Of blank blue miles, where scallops of sunlight
Skim the eye, and perhaps a boat
Tastefully bobs from bay to bay.
But watching, under the folding swell,
The slow, immensely patient body
Flex its muscles, he feels his head
Grow giddy with wheeling gulls.

Half a day out, the passenger leans
Over the rails, as the liner throbs
Its scheduled way across fair weather,
Stitching a herring-bone hem on glass.
Master of deck-games and nautical terms,
Serenely he rides — till the clouting waves
Abolish dances and close down the bar.
Hunched in his bunk then, he hears the veneer
Crack in the pitching state-rooms.

The floating bather, flatly pinned
Against the sea, squints at the sky,
Enjoying a calm sensation of poise.
He cannot gauge, on the thin border
Of air and water, what leeway he makes,
Or feel the fingering currents pass
His body along. Already his feet
Are softly dissolving. Enclosing tides
Make straight for his splayed bones.

Goggle-eyed, the diver flashes
Down through sunlight into darkness —
Quick as a fish with his rubber feet,
His streamlined body piercing the flows.
Feelers reach from the weedbed, to time
His bottled pulse; fish-eyes follow

His acrobatics, unimpressed,
Seeing, strapped to his black back,
The limits of his affinity.

Cartwheeling down the endless fathoms,
Unwrapping through his slow descent,
The drowning man escapes comparisons.
Clifftop walker, passenger, bather,
Diver — he sees them all as they were:
Alien phantoms, long marooned
Out of their element. Gladly he feels
His lungs flood with knowledge, his mind
Sprout prehistoric gills.

REVIVAL

Nothing escapes me: lying here, under the wrappings
With feet and hands raised to a peak, I share
Each twitch of twilight, can sense the surrounding air
Set gelatine thick with the sweetness of wallflowers,
 trapping
Drifts of seeds in its finely meshed snare.

Each precious detail homes to my cool tent —
The ringdove gloating in the wood, the tethered rose
Folding itself into sleep; moonlight which glows
Blue in blowball mantles; a dry adjustment
Of wingbones in the snagged and winding hedgerow.

Butterflies wink on my eyelids, wings revive
My sluggish heart. Slowly, whole landscapes infect
Each stretch of tissue. Already I can detect
The lapdog shifting beneath my heels — the live
Tickle of beard across my marble gullet.